'Reading the Bible is one of the highest joys in the Christian life. We know that, just as John Calvin did before us. This small study on Genesis is like reading the Bible with John Calvin alongside us in the room. The great French reformer trains us to be careful apprentices to Scripture, and as we do so, we enjoy seeing Christ and all his benefits wonderfully held out to us in the gospel.'

Mark Earngey,
Head of Church History, Moore Theological College,
Sydney

REFLECTING ON...

Genesis

with
John Calvin

Lee Gatiss

Scripture with the Saints
Reading the Bible with faithful believers across the ages

Reflecting on Genesis with John Calvin
Scripture with the Saints

© Church Society 2025
Second edition with corrections 2026
Church Society
Ground Floor, Centre Block
Hille Business Estate,
132 St Albans Road
Watford WD24 4AE, UK
Tel +44 (0)1923 255410

www.churchsociety.org
admin@churchsociety.org

Unless otherwise stated, all Scripture quotations are taken from The Holy Bible, New International Version. Copyright © 1973, 1978, 1984, 2011 by Biblica, Inc. Used by permission. All rights reserved.

All rights reserved. Except as may be permitted by the Copyright Act, no part of this publication may be reproduced in any form or by any means without prior permission from the publisher.

Readers are reminded that the views expressed in this book do not necessarily represent those of Church Society.

Some of the studies in this book first appeared in *90 Days in Genesis, Exodus, Psalms, and Galatians with Calvin, Luther, Bullinger and Cranmer* by Lee Gatiss (Good Book Company, 2017).

Printed in the UK
ISBN: 978-1-0685705-3-7

Series Preface

Remember your leaders, who spoke the word of God to you. Consider the outcome of their way of life and imitate their faith. Jesus Christ is the same yesterday and today and forever. Do not be carried away by all kinds of strange teachings.

– Hebrews 13:7–9

The writer to the Hebrews encourages his listeners to remember their former Christian leaders who taught them the gospel and lived it out. We are urged elsewhere to honour our current spiritual guides (e.g. 1 Thessalonians 5:12–13), but here it seems to be former pastors that are in mind. As John Calvin (1509–1564) said, 'they who have begotten us in Christ ought to be to us in the place as it were of fathers', especially if they persevered to the end. So we are to imitate the way of life of these fathers in the faith and consider the outcome of their lives.

One good thing about learning from those who spoke the word of God and guided the church in the past is that we need have no fear that they will suddenly turn out to be rogues. Every generation has those who at a certain point swerve from the truth and upset the faith of some (see 2 Timothy 2:16–18). But we can see what the outcome of our fathers' way of life and teaching was, and how they served the same Saviour and Lord as we do today.

In an age which loves novelty, it is stabilising to consider the teaching and example of the saints who came before us. It can inoculate us against the strange teachings which vie for our attention in our own time, and help us to feed on more wholesome food. It can stir us up, correct us, rebuke us, and help us live out the unchanging gospel. This is not to commend superstitious devotion to the saints or romantic antiquarianism. Rather, it is to take seriously the charge to 'remember your leaders, who spoke the word of God to you.'

That's why in this series of short books we will be reflecting on the Bible together with trustworthy guides from church history who spoke the word of God. They will teach us, build us up in our ancient common faith, and bring the wisdom of the past into our daily lives. The word of God did not originate with us, and we are not the only ones it has reached! (1 Corinthians 14:36).

So I pray you will feel connected to your own spiritual family history as you sit down to study the Scriptures with some of the best guides from our past. They may see things in God's word which you had never noticed before. They may challenge you in ways you don't expect. And all they want in return is for you to follow Jesus Christ, who is the same yesterday, today, and forever – as they did.

How to use this book

Each day, this book gives you a passage of Scripture itself to read, and some questions to think about after you have done so. You will need your Bible open! It is good to reflect on what you have read in the word first, before moving on to see what others have said about it. Only after that will we have some guidance to ponder from our historical teacher. Their words are valuable only as they illuminate the unerring word of God itself and help us apply it to ourselves.

Following this, there will be some questions of application to think about. Spend some time meditating on how you can apply the word of God to your own life, in the light of what you have learned.

Finally, it is good to turn all this into prayer back to God. Spend some time talking to him about the lessons you learn in each day's reading. This will help you digest what you read and make it a part of your own walk with God.

There is a blank page after each day's feast, for you to record any reflections of your own, either in words or diagrams or drawings, as you feel led – whatever helps you remember and respond to the living word. What struck you most forcefully? What are you not sure about? What changes might this demand of you? How would you sum it all up? What should you pray for? In this way, this little book will also become a journal of your own daily dealings with God.

I hope you will feel invigorated, challenged, comforted, and urged on in your Christian life by reading Scripture with the saints. And most of all, that you will enjoy getting to know Christ better and growing in your love and appreciation for him.

LEE GATISS
Series Editor

John Calvin

John Calvin (1509–1564) was born in the French town of Noyon, and educated at the University of Paris. He fled France in 1535 and eventually settled in Geneva, having become a Protestant. 'I was determined to study in privacy in some obscure place,' he wrote in his commentary on the Psalms some years later. But William Farel eventually persuaded him to stay and help him reform the church in Geneva. Calvin reports him saying, 'that God would surely curse my peace if I held back from giving help at a time of such great need.'

His most famous work is his *Institutes of the Christian Religion*, a highly influential book of systematic theology which he revised and enlarged several times between 1536 and 1559. But he was also a prolific preacher, wrote commentaries on almost all the books of the Bible, founded an academy for the training of pastors and church planters, and reformed the church government and liturgy of Geneva.

Many of Calvin's works were translated into English during his lifetime. The extracts from his commentary on Genesis featured here are edited and adapted from the nineteenth-century translations by John King in the twenty-two-volume edition of Calvin's commentaries.

※ Day 1 ※

In the Beginning

GENESIS 1:1–19

The world was created by God out of nothing. It is good and wonderful.

Read Genesis 1:1–19

What do you admire most about the design of God's creation?

What is the difference between Genesis 1 and a modern scientific textbook?

Admiring God's Works

'God saw that the light was good' (verse 4). Here God is introduced by Moses as surveying his work, that he might take pleasure in it. But he does it for our sake, to teach us that God has made nothing without a certain reason and design. And we ought not so to

understand the words of Moses as if God did not know that his work was good until it was finished. But the meaning of the passage is that the work, such as we now see it, was approved by God. Therefore nothing remains for us, but to agree with this judgment of God. And this admonition is very useful. For we ought to apply all our senses to the admiring contemplation of the works of God.

The Miracle of Clouds

'Let there be a vault/expanse' (verse 6). We see clouds suspended in the air, which threaten to fall upon our heads, yet leave us space to breathe. Those who deny that this is effected by the wonderful providence of God are vainly inflated with the folly of their own minds. We know indeed that the rain is naturally produced; but the deluge sufficiently shows how speedily we might be overwhelmed by the bursting of the clouds, if the cataracts of heaven were not closed by the hand of God.

Astronomy is Good

'God made two great lights' (verse 16). Moses wrote in a popular style things which, without instruction, all ordinary persons endued with common sense are able to understand. But astronomers investigate with great labour whatever the intelligence of the human mind can comprehend. Nevertheless, this study is not to be rejected, nor this science to be condemned because some frantic persons boldly reject whatever is unknown to them. For astronomy is not only pleasant, but also very useful to be known. It cannot be denied that this art unfolds the admirable wisdom of God. Wherefore, as ingenious people who have expended useful

labour on this subject are to be honoured, so they who have leisure and capacity ought not to neglect this kind of exercise.

Apply

Next time you go outside, ponder how amazing it is that the clouds don't suddenly burst and fall upon you!

What other miracles of providence in the design of creation do you admire?

Pray

Thank God for the natural sciences that we use to investigate his admirable wisdom and design in creation.

Ask God to help you understand and appreciate those aspects of creation that you may previously have taken for granted.

Notes and prayers

�֍ Day 2 ✦

God Blesses Mankind

Genesis 1:20–31

God made mankind and blessed them. In the symmetry of God's works there is the highest perfection, to which nothing can be added.

Read Genesis 1:20–31

What is the place of humanity in God's creation?

What does God provide for them?

God takes counsel with himself

'Let us make mankind' (verse 26). With these words, God 'takes counsel' and discusses the creation of mankind in his image. By doing so, he commends to our attention the dignity of our nature, and testifies that he is about to undertake something great

and wonderful. But since the Lord needs no other counsellor, there can be no doubt that he consulted with himself. Christians, therefore, properly contend, from this testimony, that there exists a plurality of Persons in the Godhead. God summons no foreign counsellor.

The image of God

'In our image' (verse 26). It is too crude to say that our resemblance to God is to be found simply in the shape or form of the human body, as some people think. Others proceed with a little more subtlety, and maintain that the image of God is in the human body because in it God's admirable workmanship shines brightly. But this opinion is by no means in accordance with Scripture. Others see God's image in the dominion which was given to mankind in order that they might, in a certain sense, act as God's representative in the government of the world; but they are not correct either. This is only a very small part of what it means to be made in the image of God.

Since the image of God was destroyed in us by the Fall, we may judge from its restoration what it originally had been. Paul says that we are transformed into the image of God *by the gospel*. And, according to him, spiritual regeneration is nothing else than the restoration of God's image in us (see Colossians 3:10 and Ephesians 4:23–24).

God's Blessing

'God blessed them' (verse 28). God certainly did not intend that mankind should be slenderly and sparingly sustained; but rather, by these words, he promises a liberal abundance, which should leave nothing lacking for a sweet and pleasant life. For Moses relates how generous the Lord had been to them, in bestowing on them all things which they could desire, that their ingratitude might have the less excuse. After the workmanship of the world had received the last finishing touch, God pronounces it perfectly good.

Apply

Do you agree that there are hints of more than one 'Person' in the Godhead, in Genesis 1?

Ponder the fact that God has given us 'a liberal abundance' of good things in creation, for a sweet and pleasant life.

Pray

Thank God for his goodness in creating humanity, male and female, in his own image.

Praise God for the wonderful blessings he has given us, even in this fallen world.

Notes and Prayers

❊ DAY 3 ❊

God's Rest

GENESIS 2:1–3

God did not cease from the work of creating the world until he had completed it in every part, so that nothing should be lacking in its suitable abundance. But on the seventh day, he rested.

Read Genesis 2:1–3

Why do some people think that God may have created the world and set it going but then left it to its own devices?

What should we be doing with the Lord's Day (Revelation 1:10), once a week?

The Meaning of God Resting

The question may not improperly be put, what kind of rest this was. For it is certain that since God sustains the world by his power, governs it by his providence, cherishes and even propagates all creatures, he is constantly at work. Therefore that saying of

Christ is true, that the Father and he himself had worked from the beginning (John 5:17), because, if God should but withdraw his hand a little, all things would immediately perish and dissolve into nothing, as is declared in Psalm 104:29. The last touch of God had been put on his creation, in order that nothing might be lacking in the perfection of the world. We must not infer that God so ceased from his works as to desert them, since they only flourish and subsist in him.

A Special Day

God sanctifies the seventh day when he renders it illustrious, that by a special law it may be distinguished from the rest. God always had respect to the welfare of people. His benediction is nothing else than a solemn consecration, by which God claims for himself the meditations and employments of people on the seventh day. This is, indeed, the proper business of the whole life, in which people should daily exercise themselves, to consider the infinite goodness, justice, power, and wisdom of God, in this magnificent theatre of heaven and earth. But, in case people should prove less diligently attentive to it than they ought, every seventh day has been especially selected for the purpose of supplying what was lacking in daily meditation.

God dedicated every seventh day to rest, that his own example might be a perpetual rule. God did not command people simply to have a holiday every seventh day, as if he delighted in their laziness; but rather that they, being released from all other business, might the more readily apply their minds to the Creator of the world. For God cannot either more gently allure, or more effectually incite us to obedience, than by inviting and exhorting us to the imitation of himself.

Apply

How would it change the way you see the world to realise that God is sustaining every aspect of it, each second, and has not deserted it?

Are you using your Sunday rest for laziness or for meditating on God's infinite goodness, justice, power, and wisdom?

Pray

Thank God for the 'magnificent theatre of heaven and earth' he created which, though spoiled by sin, is sustained by him each day.

Ask God who 'claims for himself the meditations and employments of people on the seventh day' to help you better use each Lord's day for him.

Notes and prayers

✳ Day 4 ✳

Man and Wife

Genesis 2:18–25

There are many difficulties in our relationships, which are the fruits of our fallen nature, but some residue of God's original good design remains.

Read Genesis 2:18–25

Why did God make Eve (verses 18, 20)?

Do you think this was just a one-off, or the start of an ongoing pattern?

Alone

'It is not good for the man to be alone' (verse 18). Moses now explains the design of God in creating woman – namely, that there should be human beings on the earth who might cultivate mutual society between themselves. Man was formed to be a social animal. The human race could not exist without the woman.

Although God pronounced, concerning Adam, that it would not be profitable for him to be alone, yet I do not restrict this declaration to him alone, but rather regard it as a common law of our vocation. So everyone ought to receive it as said to them, that solitude is not good, though there are some who are able by God's grace to remain single (see 1 Corinthians 7).

Together

'I will make a helper suitable for him' (verse 18). There is a vulgar proverb which says woman is a necessary evil. But the voice of God is rather to be heard, which declares that woman is given as a companion and an associate to the man, to assist him to live well.

In the current corrupt state of mankind, this blessing of God is neither perceived nor flourishes. But if the integrity of man had remained to this day such as it was from the beginning, that divine institution would be clearly discerned, and the sweetest harmony would reign in marriage. The husband would look up with reverence to God, the woman would be a faithful assistant to him in this, and both with one consent would cultivate a holy, a friendly, and a peaceful relationship.

Now, it has happened by our fault and by the corruption of nature that this happiness of marriage has in a great measure perished or, at least, is mixed and infected with many inconveniences. Hence arise strifes, troubles, sorrows, disagreement and discord, and a boundless sea of evils. Still, marriage was not capable of being so far spoiled by our depravity that the blessing which God has once sanctioned by his word should be utterly abolished and extinguished. Therefore, some residue of divine good remains, like when a fire is apparently smothered, but some sparks still glitter.

Apply

What do you think it means for us to be 'social animals'?

Calvin rejects a vulgar proverb and says we should listen to God's word instead. What other worldly sayings or attitudes about male-female relationships need correcting?

Pray

Thank God for all the relationships you have in life which mean you are not entirely alone (especially for your wife or husband, if you have one).

Ask God to help you cultivate holy, friendly, and peaceful relationships that will help others 'look up with reverence to God'.

Notes and Prayers

✳ Day 5 ✳

The Fall

Genesis 3:1–7

Pride was the beginning of all evils, and by proudly rejecting God's word in monstrous ingratitude, the human race was enslaved to the devil.

Read Genesis 3:1–7

In what ways do you think sin is a rejection of God's ordering for creation?

What do you think was the essence of Adam and Eve's sin?

The World Turned Upside Down

In this chapter, Moses explains that man, after he had been deceived by Satan, revolted from his maker. He became entirely changed and so degenerate that the image of God, in which he had been formed, was obliterated. Moses then declares that the whole world fell together with him and that much of its original excellence was destroyed.

The baseness of human ingratitude is more clearly perceived in this: that although Adam and Eve knew that all animals were given by the hand of God into subjection to them (Genesis 1:26), they allowed themselves to be led away by one of their own slaves into rebellion against God. As often as they saw any one of the animals which were in the world, they ought to have been reminded of the supreme authority and singular goodness of God. But, on the contrary, when they saw the serpent in rebellion against his Creator, not only did they neglect to punish it but in violation of all lawful order they subjected and devoted themselves to it. They became participators in the same rebellion. What can be imagined more dishonourable than this extreme depravity?

The design of Moses, therefore, was to show in a few words how greatly our present condition differs from our original state in creation. He wished us to learn, with humble confession of our fault, to lament our evils.

Forsaking God's Word

What was the sin of Adam and Eve? They revolted from God, when, having forsaken his word, they lent their ears to the falsehoods of Satan. From this we infer that God will be seen and adored in his word and, therefore, that all reverence for him is shaken off when his word is despised. The word of God obtains its due honour only with a few, but some rush onward with impunity in contempt of this word, and still assign to themselves a chief rank among the worshippers of God. But God does not manifest himself to us otherwise than through the word. So, unbelief was the root of defection; just as faith alone unites us to God.

Apply

Are you tempted to reject or marginalise God's word in favour of some other voices in your decision-making processes?

By subjecting themselves to an animal, Adam and Eve overturned the order God had made for them in the garden. In what ways does your personal sin subvert the way things were designed by God in his goodness to be?

Pray

Ask God to help you understand more of the depths of sin and what it has done to the world.

Confess to God your own disbelief and rejection of his word.

Notes and Prayers

✷ Day 6 ✷

Sin Exposed

GENESIS 3:8–24

Adam and Eve aggravate their crime with frivolous and ungodly defences and so, along with the serpent, they are judged by God.

Read Genesis 3:8–24

How do Adam and Eve try to hide and excuse their sin?

Why does God bar the way back to the tree of life (verse 24)?

Flimsy Leaves

Verse 8. As soon as the voice of God sounds, Adam and Eve perceive that the leaves by which they thought themselves well protected are of no avail. The difference between good and evil is engraved on the hearts of all, as Paul teaches (Romans 2:15). But all bury the disgrace of their vices under flimsy leaves until God, by his voice, inwardly strikes their consciences. Hence, after God had shaken them out of their dullness, their alarmed consciences compelled them to hear his voice.

Dreadful Alienation

Verse 17. The Lord determined that his anger should, like a deluge, overflow all parts of the earth. So wherever man might look, the atrocity of his sin should meet his eyes. Before the fall, the state of the world was a most fair and delightful mirror of the divine favour and paternal indulgence towards mankind. Now, in all the elements we perceive that we are cursed. And although (as David says) the earth is still full of the mercy of God (Psalm 33:5), yet, at the same time, there appear manifest signs of his dreadful alienation from us. If we are unmoved by these, then we betray our blindness and indifference. Only, so that sadness and horror should not overwhelm us, the Lord sprinkles everywhere the tokens of his goodness.

Excommunicated

Verses 22–24. By depriving Adam and Eve of the symbol (the tree of life), God also takes away the thing signified by it. A solemn excommunication is pronounced so that they would understand themselves to be deprived of their former life. It was not that the Lord would cut them off from all hope of salvation, but he did not want them to entertain a vain hope of the perpetuity of the life they had lost. They could not actually enjoy life against the will of God, even if they devoured the whole tree of life. There never was any intrinsic effectiveness in the tree. But by taking it away, he wanted them to seek new assistance elsewhere. They could only recover life by the death of Christ.

Apply

Do you blame others for your own sin, as Adam and Eve tried to transfer blame?

What signs of the curse, and signs of God's mercy, do you see in the world today?

Pray

Thank God that in his righteous anger against sin he remains gracious and merciful.

Ask God to give you an understanding of sin and judgment that leads to greater humility and repentance.

Notes and prayers

❋ Day 7 ❋

Cain and Abel

Genesis 4:1–16

Since the whole human race is rejected by God after the Fall, there is no other way of reconciliation to divine favour than through God-given faith.

Read Genesis 4:1–16

Why do you think God accepted Abel's offering (verse 4)?

Why do you think God did not accept Cain's offering (verse 5)?

Abel and his Offering

Verse 4. The writer of Hebrews says Abel's sacrifice was accepted by faith (Hebrews 11:4). Filled with the good odour of faith, it had a sweet-smelling aroma to God. Moses does not simply state that the worship which Abel had paid was pleasing to God, but he begins with the *person* of the offerer (verse 4). By this he signifies that God will regard no works with favour unless the one who does them has already been accepted and approved by him. And no wonder; for 'people look at the outward appearance, but the LORD looks at the heart' (1 Samuel 16:7). Therefore, he only assesses works as they proceed from the fountain of the heart.

This is why he not only rejects but abhors the sacrifices of the wicked, however splendid they may appear in the eyes of men. All works done before faith, whatever splendour of righteousness may appear in them, are nothing but mere sins, being defiled from their roots. They are offensive to the Lord, whom nothing can please without inward purity of heart. For this must be received as a settled point – in the judgment of God, no respect is had to works until someone is received into his favour. Moreover, since faith is a gracious gift of God, and a special illumination of the Spirit, then it is easy to infer that his mere grace goes before us, just as if he had raised us from the dead.

Cain and his Offering

Verse 5. Cain conducted himself as hypocrites are accustomed to do. He wished to appease God, as one discharging a debt, by external sacrifices, without the least intention of dedicating himself to God. But this is true worship, to offer ourselves as spiritual sacrifices to God. When God sees such hypocrisy, combined with gross and manifest mockery of himself, it is not surprising that he hates it, and is unable to bear it. For it is his will, first to have us devoted to himself; he then seeks our works in testimony of our obedience to him, but only in the second place.

Apply

Have you ever tried to 'appease God, as one discharging a debt' without being truly devoted to God?

Romans 8:8 says that 'those who are in the realm of the flesh cannot please God'. How do you feel about this idea?

Pray

Ask God to help you love and trust him sincerely from the heart.

Ask God to help you show your heartfelt love for him in appropriately obedient ways.

Notes and prayers

※ Day 8 ※

The Flood

GENESIS 6:5–8

God was neither too harsh nor too hasty in exacting punishment from the wicked people of the world.

Read Genesis 6:5–8

Why do you think the description of human sin is so lavish?

What does it mean here for God to grieve and be sorry that he made us (verses 6–7)?

The Lord Saw

God was not induced to destroy the world merely for a slight cause. 'The Lord saw', (verse 5) indicates long-continued patience. God did not proclaim his sentence to destroy humanity until he had well observed and long considered their case, and saw them to be past recovery. A vast wickedness reigned everywhere, so that the whole earth was covered with it. And so we perceive that it was not overwhelmed with a deluge of waters until it had first been immersed in the pollution of wickedness.

Continual Depravity

Wickedness was too deeply seated in people's hearts to leave any hope of repentance. Moses teaches us that the mind of humanity was thoroughly saturated with sin. The world had then become so hardened in its wickedness, and was so far from any amendment or from entertaining any feeling of penitence, that it grew worse and worse as time advanced. This was not the folly of a few days, but the habitual depravity which the children transmitted from their parents to their descendants. This is not a mere complaint concerning a few men, but a description of the human mind when left to itself, destitute of the Spirit of God.

God's Heart

Moses introduces God as speaking in a human way, by a figure of speech which ascribes human affections to God. Certainly God is not sorrowful or sad, but remains forever in his celestial and happy repose. Yet because it could not otherwise be known how great is God's hatred and detestation of sin, therefore the Spirit accommodates himself to our capacity. There is no need for us to involve ourselves in thorny and difficult questions. It is obvious that these words of repentance and grief are used to teach us that God was so offended by the atrocious wickedness of mankind, as if they had wounded his heart with mortal grief. In order more effectually to pierce our hearts, he clothes himself with our affections. So unless we wish to provoke God, and to put him to grief, let us learn to abhor and to flee from sin.

Apply

Are your feelings about sin in your heart and in the world the same as those God is represented as having here?

Do you really think that human sin is as bad as Moses makes it out to be?

Pray

Confess to God the evil intentions and thoughts of your own heart.

Thank God that he has saved you by grace alone, despite your sin.

Notes and Prayers

�֍ Day 9 ✶

The Tower of Babel

GENESIS 11:1–9

As soon as mortals are inflated above measure, they wage war with God. But the division of languages is inflicted as a punishment for their conspiracy.

Read Genesis 11:1–9

What was it that drove them to build the tower (verse 4)?

Why do you think God chose to punish them in this particular way?

Proud Contempt

Some people speculate that the tower of Babel was built as a refuge and protection in case God should determine to overwhelm the earth with a deluge again. But they have no other guide, that

I can see, but the dream of their own brain. For Moses says no such thing. Rather, he speaks of their mad ambitions and proud contempt of God. They wish to have an immortal name on earth; and thus they build, as if in opposition to the will of God. Ambition not only does injury to mankind, but exalts itself even against God, waging war against him. To build a tower was not in itself so great a crime; but to raise an eternal monument to themselves, which might endure throughout all ages, was a proof of headstrong pride, joined with contempt of God.

Earthly Ambition

Moses intimates that they had not been induced to commence this work on account of the ease with which it could be accomplished nor on account of any other advantages. Rather, they contended with great and arduous difficulties, by which means their guilt became more aggravated. They wear themselves out in vain on a difficult and laborious enterprise, and like madmen they rush impetuously against God. Difficulty often deters us from necessary works; but these people, when they had neither stones nor mortar, do not hesitate to attempt the raising of an edifice which may transcend the clouds. We are taught therefore to what length people's lust will hurry them, when they indulge their ambition. This is the perpetual infatuation of the world: to neglect heaven, and to seek immortality on earth, where everything is fading and temporary.

Disgrace

God declares that he is at perpetual war with the unmeasured audacity of men; anything we undertake without his approval will end miserably. People had already been spread abroad, and this ought not to be regarded as a punishment. But now the principal bond of conjunction between them was cut. Behold what they gained by their foolish ambition to acquire a name! He brands them with eternal disgrace.

Apply

What is it that drives your own ambitions?

Are your ambitions merely earthly, 'where everything is fading and temporary'?

Pray

Confess to God where your ambitions in life have been driven by personal pride.

Ask God to give you godly ambitions which serve his kingdom and glory more than your own.

Notes and prayers

※ Day 10 ※

The Call of Abram

Genesis 12:1–3

God calls Abram (later to be called Abraham), who was worshipping other gods, to leave his former life and be blessed by giving up everything to follow the true God.

Read Genesis 12:1–3

Why do you think God chooses to bless Abram?

Why does this blessing come with a command to leave everything else behind?

Gracious Call

Abram's calling is an instance of the gracious mercy of God. We must always recall (see Joshua 24:2) that Abram was plunged in the filth of idolatry. And now God freely stretches forth his hand to bring back the wanderer. He deigns to open his sacred mouth that he may show to one deceived by Satan's schemes the way of salvation.

It is wonderful that a man, miserable and lost, should have the covenant of life placed in his possession, and he himself constituted the father of all the faithful. But this is done with a deliberate design, in order that the grace of God might be more conspicuously revealed. For Abram is an example of the calling of us all, that by the mere mercy of God things which are 'nothing' are raised up to be 'something'.

The Test of Faith

The sweetness of their native soil holds nearly all people bound to itself, so God strenuously persists in his command to 'leave your country'. He does this to thoroughly penetrate the mind of Abram, who is still more deeply affected when he hears that he must renounce his kindred and his father's house. Yet it is not to be supposed that God takes a cruel pleasure in the trouble of his servants; but he thus tries all their affections, that he may not leave any lurking-places undiscovered in their hearts.

We see many persons zealous for a short time, who afterwards become frozen. Why is this, but because they build without a foundation? Therefore God determined thoroughly to rouse all Abram's senses, that he might undertake nothing rashly, lest, changing his mind soon afterwards, he should veer with the wind and return.

Therefore, if we desire to follow God with constancy, it is good for us carefully to meditate on all the inconveniences, difficulties and dangers which await us. A hasty zeal may produce fading flowers, but from a deep and well-fixed root of piety we may bring forth fruit in our whole life.

Apply

Do you sometimes think that God chose you because of something great or good about you?

What has God asked you to leave behind or abandon to follow him?

Pray

Praise God that he chose us to follow him despite the fact that we were 'nothing', or even that we were against him.

Ask God to help you follow him wholeheartedly, whatever you may have to leave behind.

Notes and Prayers

※ Day 11 ※

Abram's Shield and Reward

Genesis 15

The one who has God himself for their inheritance does not exult in fading joy, but enjoys the solid happiness of eternal life by embracing God as their Father.

Read Genesis 15

What does God promise to Abram in this passage?

What does verse 6 mean by 'credited it to him as righteousness'?

Our Reward

In calling himself Abram's 'reward' (verse 1), God teaches Abram to be satisfied with himself alone. By this voice, God daily speaks to all his faithful ones. Having once undertaken to defend us, he will take care to preserve us in safety under his hand and to protect us by his power. God also ascribes to himself the office of a shield, to make himself the protector of our salvation. So we should not be excessively fearful in any dangers.

Since people surrounded with innumerable desires of the flesh are at times unstable, and too much addicted to the love of the present life, God declares that he alone is sufficient for the perfection of a happy life to the faithful. It ought to be deeply engraved on our minds that in God alone we have the highest and complete perfection of all good things.

We shall be truly happy when God is propitious to us. For he not only pours upon us the abundance of his kindness, but offers himself to us, that we may enjoy him. Now what is there more which people can desire when they really enjoy God?

Whoever is fully persuaded that their life is protected by the hand of God, and that they can never be miserable while God is gracious to them, will find the best remedy for all evils. Not that the faithful can be entirely free from fear and care, as long as they are tossed by the tempests of this life; but because the storm is hushed in their own breast, faith triumphs over fear.

Credited to him as Righteousness

The faith of Abram is commended, because by it he embraced the promise of God. It is also commended because by it Abram obtained righteousness in the sight of God, and that by imputation. Just as we understand that they to whom sin is imputed are guilty before God, so those to whom he imputes righteousness are approved by him as just. So Abram was received into the number and rank of the just by the imputation of righteousness.

Apply

What do you think you need to be truly happy?

Do you think of knowing God himself as the greatest blessing you have, or are you more fixated on the other things he gives you?

Pray

Praise God that he has given us himself, as our shield and reward.

Ask God to help you look to him more and more for your happiness, rather than to your secret sins and desires.

NOTES AND PRAYERS

✻ Day 12 ✻

Escape from Sodom

Genesis 19:12–26

The faithful ought to endeavour with greater earnestness to prepare themselves to follow God and beware lest with deaf ears they disregard his warnings.

Read Genesis 19:12–26

Lot was the nephew of Abram, now called Abraham. Why do you think Lot was so slow in leaving the city he knew was about to be destroyed?

Why was Lot's wife turned into a pillar of salt?

Read 2 Peter 2:7. How does the Bible view Lot, flawed though he was?

Lot's Sloth

Having praised the faith and piety of Lot, Moses shows that something human still adhered to him; because the angels hastened him, when he was lingering. A multiplicity of cares and fears disturb his anxious mind. He does not consider that he must act like persons shipwrecked, who, in order that they may come safe into port, cast their cargo into the sea. He does not doubt that God is speaking the truth, nor does he refuse to go; but entangled with many cares, he who ought to have run hastily and without delay, moves with slow and halting pace.

Here the Spirit of God presents to us, as in a mirror, our own tardiness – in order that we, shaking off all sloth, may prepare ourselves for prompt obedience, as soon as the heavenly voice sounds in our ears.

The Lord's Hand

It is often necessary for us to be forcibly drawn away from scenes which we do not willingly leave. Riches, honours, or other things of that kind may prove an obstacle to many. So if they are robbed of their fortune, or reduced to a lower rank, let them realise that the Lord has laid hold of their hand because words and exhortations had not sufficiently profited them. The mercy of God struggled with the sluggishness of Lot. Left to himself, he would, by lingering, have brought down upon his own head the destruction which was already near.

Lot's Wife

Lot's wife was moved by some evil desire; she did not cheerfully leave Sodom to hasten to the place where God called her. Christ commands us to remember Lot's wife (Luke 17:32), lest the allurements of the world should draw us aside from meditation on the heavenly life. It is therefore probable that she, being discontented with the favour God had granted her, glided into unholy desires, of which thing also her tardiness was a sign.

They sin no less grievously, who, being delivered not from Sodom but from hell, fix their eyes on some other object than the prize of their high calling.

Apply

What cares and fears prevent you from moving more earnestly in the direction you know God wants you to go?

What allurements of this world are distracting you and making you discontent with God?

Pray

Confess to God your sluggish obedience to his word.

Ask God to help you keep your mind focused on the city to come, whose 'architect and builder' is God himself.

Notes and Prayers

✻ Day 13 ✻

The Binding of Isaac

GENESIS 22:1–19

God tests the faith which Abraham has placed in his word, by a counter-assault of the word itself, which seemed to threaten the whole salvation of the world.

Read Genesis 22:1–19

Beyond the sheer horror of Abraham killing his own son, why would the death of Isaac be such a huge problem for Abraham and his story?

How do you think Abraham resolved any conflicts in his mind here?

Abraham's Faith

Not only is the death of his son announced to him, but Abraham is commanded with his own hand to slay him. It is as if he were required not only to throw aside but to cut in pieces or cast into the fire the charter of his salvation, and to have nothing left for himself but death and hell. But it may be asked how, under the guidance of faith, he could be brought to sacrifice his son, seeing that what was proposed to him was in opposition to that word of God on which it is necessary for faith to rely (Genesis 17:19; 21:12)?

To this question the writer of Hebrews answers, that Abraham's confidence in the word of God remained unshaken. He hoped that God would be able to cause the promised blessing to spring up, even out of the dead ashes of his son (Hebrews 11:17–19). His mind, however, must of necessity have been severely crushed and violently agitated when the *command* and the *promise* of God were conflicting within him.

Although he did not immediately discover how the contradiction might be removed he, nevertheless, by hope, reconciled the command with the promise. Being persuaded that God was faithful, he left the unknown issue to divine providence.

Abraham's Example

It remains for every one of us to apply this example to ourselves. The Lord, indeed, is so indulgent to our weakness that he does not thus severely and sharply try our faith. Yet he intended, in the father of all the faithful, to propose an example by which he might call us to a general trial of faith. For faith, which is more precious than gold and silver, ought not to lie idle without trial (1 Peter 1:7).

Experience teaches that each will be tried by God, according to the measure of their faith. At the same time also we may observe that God tests his servants, not only when he subdues the affections of the flesh, but when he reduces all their senses to nothing, that he may lead them to a complete renunciation of themselves.

Apply

Would you trust and obey, if God's word commanded you to do something but you didn't understand how it would work out?

What do you think is the most difficult test of faith which God might ask of you?

Pray

Praise God that he provided a ram in place of Isaac, and the sacrifice of his own Son, Jesus, on the cross in our place.

Ask God to give you strength to trust and obey him, whatever comes your way.

NOTES AND PRAYERS

✢ Day 14 ✢

Esau Despises his Birthright

Genesis 25:19–34

Jacob exploits Esau's weakness to acquire his treasured rights of inheritance as the firstborn son, but Esau is condemned for treating that spiritual blessing with such contempt.

Read Genesis 25:19–34

Esau should have had priority in inheriting the promise and blessing to Abraham, so why does God say 'the elder will serve the younger' (verse 23)?

Esau exchanges his precious spiritual birthright for some bread and lentil stew. What does this reveal about his way of thinking?

Earthly vs. Spiritual Good

In desiring and asking for food, Esau commits nothing worthy of condemnation; but when he says, 'I am about to die! What good is the birthright to me?' he betrays a profane desire entirely addicted to the earth and to the flesh. In order to escape immediate death, he exchanges his birthright for food; but he grievously sins in doing so, because he regards his birthright as of no value, unless it may be made profitable in the present life. For he barters a spiritual for an earthly and fading good.

Esau's Godlessness

On this account, the New Testament calls him a 'godless person' (Hebrews 12:16) as one who settles in the present life, and will not aspire higher. But it would have been his true wisdom rather to undergo a thousand deaths than to renounce his birthright; which, so far from being confined within the narrow limits of one age alone, was capable of transmitting the perpetuity of a heavenly life to his posterity also.

Now, let each of us look carefully to themselves; for since the disposition of us all is earthly, if we follow nature as our leader, we shall easily renounce the celestial inheritance. Therefore, we should frequently recall to mind the Apostle's exhortation, 'Let us not be godless as Esau was.'

Esau, having satisfied his appetite, did not consider that he had sacrificed a blessing far more valuable than a hundred lives, to purchase a meal which would be over in half an hour. Thus are all godless persons accustomed to act: alienated from the celestial life, they do not perceive that they have lost anything, till God thunders upon them out of heaven. As long as they enjoy their carnal wishes, they cast the anger of God behind them; and hence it happens that they go stupidly forward to their own destruction. Therefore, let us learn – if, at any time, we, being deceived by the allurements of the world, swerve from the right way – quickly to rouse ourselves from our slumber.

Apply

Are there ways in which you are prioritising your natural, carnal desires, over your 'celestial inheritance'?

How would it change your day today if you valued your spiritual blessings higher than your earthly comforts?

Pray

Praise God that you are saved, not by works but because of God's choice before you were born or had done anything either good or bad (see Romans 9:11–12 which quotes Genesis 25:23).

Ask God to help you so value the eternal blessings you have in Christ, that you will not throw them away for anything as cheap and temporary as a bowl of lentils.

Notes and Prayers

✸ Day 15 ✸

Isaac Blesses Jacob

GENESIS 27:1–29

God allowed Isaac to be deceived, in order to show that it was not by the will of man that Jacob was raised up.

Read Genesis 27:1–29

Why do you think Moses spends so long telling this almost childish story of deception?

Did God bless Jacob because he was so clever and deceitful?

Cheating

In this chapter Moses recounts a history which does not appear to be of great utility. It amounts to this: Esau having gone out at his father's command to hunt, Jacob in his brother's clothing was, through the cunning of his mother, induced to obtain by stealth the blessing due by right to the firstborn. It seems even like child's play to present to his father a goat instead of venison, to pass himself off as hairy by putting on skins and pretending to be his brother, to get the blessing by a lie.

But Moses does not in vain pause over this narrative as a most serious matter. We must observe that when Jacob received the blessing from his father, this token confirmed to him the oracle by which the Lord had preferred him to his brother (Genesis 25:23). For the blessing here spoken of was not a mere prayer – rather, it made manifest the grace of election.

Election

The preference which God gave to Jacob over his brother Esau was not granted as a reward for his merits, neither was it obtained by his own industry. It proceeded from the mere grace of God himself. The disparity of condition certainly cannot be ascribed either to the virtue of the one or the vice of the other, seeing they were not yet born when the promise was given that 'the older shall serve the younger'.

Let it suffice us to hold fast what we gather from Paul's interpretation (Romans 9:10–13) – that whereas the whole human race deserves the same destruction, and is bound under the same sentence of condemnation, some are delivered by gracious mercy; others are justly left in their own destruction. And that those whom God has chosen are not preferred to others because God foresaw they *would* be holy, but in order that they *might* be holy. Among men some perish, some obtain salvation; but the cause of this depends on the secret will of God.

Apply

How do you react to the idea that God's will is the ultimate cause of our salvation?

Do you think that this gives us a license to behave as badly as Jacob often does in Genesis?

Pray

Praise God that he is sovereign in creation, revelation, redemption and final judgment.

Ask God to help you, as a Christian, to be in practice what he chose you to be (i.e. holy).

Notes and Prayers

※ Day 16 ※

Jacob's Ladder

Genesis 28:10–22

Christ is the mediator through whom all celestial blessings flow down to us and through whom we, in turn, ascend to God.

Read Genesis 28:10–22

What do you understand by the image of the ladder/stairway in Jacob's dream?

What is 'the house of God … the gate of heaven' (verse 17)?

The Mediator

God manifested himself as seated upon a ladder which touched heaven and earth, and which was the vehicle of angels. To us who hold that the covenant of God was founded in Christ, and that Christ himself was the eternal image of the Father in which he manifested himself to the holy patriarchs, there is nothing in this vision intricate or ambiguous.

We are alienated from God by sin, and flee from his presence. Angels, to whom is committed the guardianship of the human race, do not communicate with us in such a way that we become conscious of their presence. It is Christ alone who connects heaven and earth: he is the only mediator who reaches from heaven down to earth. Through him the fullness of all celestial blessings flows down to us; and we, in turn, ascend to God.

If, then, we say that the ladder is a figure of Christ, the exposition will not be forced. For the likeness of a ladder well suits the mediator. We feel unspeakable joy when we hear that Christ, who so far excels all creatures, is nevertheless joined with us. His friendly and lovely image is depicted, that we may know by his descent that heaven is opened to us.

The Gate of Heaven

Jacob calls that place 'the gate of heaven' (verse 17). Because God is placed in heaven as on his royal throne, Jacob truly declares that in seeing God, he had penetrated into heaven. In this sense the preaching of the gospel is called the kingdom of heaven, and the sacraments may be called the gate of heaven, because they admit us into the presence of God.

Roman Catholics foolishly misapply this passage to their temples. But even if the places which they designate by this title ('House of God') were not polluted with ungodly superstitions, yet this honour belongs to no particular place, since Christ has filled the whole world with the presence of his deity. Only those helps to faith (preaching and the sacraments) by which God raises us to himself can be called the gates of heaven.

Apply

Do you think that Calvin is right to interpret the ladder as being a picture of Christ our mediator? (See also John 1:51.)

Do you think it is right to say that no particular place can now be called 'the house of God'?

Pray

Praise and thank God for sending Jesus to be our mediator.

Ask God to help you appreciate more the blessings of gospel preaching and gospel sacraments (baptism and the Lord's Supper).

Notes and Prayers

� Day 17 ✳

Wrestling with God

GENESIS 32:22–32

The faithful become conquerors in their temptations only with the strength of God made perfect in their weakness, and by being injured and wounded in the conflict.

Read Genesis 32:22–32

Why do you think Jacob wrestled with this person?

Who do you think this person was?

Wrestling with Temptations

This vision taught Jacob that many conflicts awaited him, and that he would be the conqueror in them all. Yet there is not the least doubt that the Lord exhibited, in his person, a specimen of the temptations common to all his people which await them and must be constantly submitted to in this transitory life. So it is right to keep in view this design of the vision, which is to represent all the servants of God in this world as wrestlers, because the Lord exercises them with various kinds of conflicts.

Moreover, it is not said that Satan, or any mortal man, wrestled with Jacob, but God himself – to teach us that our faith is tried by him. Whenever we are tempted, our business is truly with him. For as all prosperity flows from his goodness, so adversity is either the rod with which he corrects our sins, or the test of our faith and patience.

We do not fight against him, except by his own power, and with his own weapons. For he, having challenged us to this contest, at the same time furnishes us with means of resistance, so that he both fights against us and for us.

God's Name

Jacob said, 'Please tell me your name'. Though his wish was pious, the Lord does not grant it, because the time of full revelation was not yet completed. For the fathers were required to walk in the twilight of morning, and the Lord manifested himself to them by degrees until, at length, Christ, the Sun of Righteousness, arose, in whom perfect brightness shines forth. Even Moses was only permitted to behold his glory from behind (Exodus 33:21–23); yet because he occupied an intermediate place between patriarchs and apostles, he is said to have seen 'face to face' the God who had been hidden from the fathers (Exodus 33:11, Deuteronomy 34:10).

But now, since God has approached more nearly unto us, our ingratitude is most ungodly and detestable, if we do not run to meet him, with ardent desire to obtain such great grace.

Apply

How much do you actually wrestle with temptations and with God in prayer about them?

Why do you think God only 'revealed himself by degrees' before Christ came?

Pray

Praise God that we can know him in Jesus, and one day will truly see him face to face.

Ask God to strengthen you in the battle with temptation, daily.

Notes and Prayers

�֎ Day 18 ✲

Joseph's Dreams

Genesis 37:1–11

As the hymn-writer William Cowper once put it, 'God moves in a mysterious way, his wonders to perform' – in the life of Joseph, and of Christ.

Read Genesis 37:1–11

Why do you think God first revealed in a dream what would eventually happen in the story of Joseph?

Was it acceptable for the brothers to be jealous of and nasty towards Joseph?

They Hated Him

The brothers conceive enmity against Joseph, whom they see to be more tenderly loved by their father. That a many-coloured coat and similar trifles inflamed them to devise a scheme of slaughter is a proof of their detestable cruelty.

Having stated what were the first seeds of this enmity, Moses now ascends higher, and shows that Joseph had been elected, by the wonderful purpose of God, to great things. God revealed in dreams what he would do, that afterwards it might be known that nothing had happened by mere luck – it had been fixed by a celestial decree, which was in its proper time carried forward through circuitous windings to its completion.

God Protected Him

The sons of Jacob conspire to put to death the very person without whom they cannot be preserved. Indeed, he who was ordained to be the minister of salvation to them is thrown into a well, and with difficulty rescued from the jaws of death. Driven about by various misfortunes, he seems to be an alien from his father's house. Afterwards, he is cast into prison, as into another tomb, where, for a long time, he languishes. Nothing, therefore, was less probable than that the family of Jacob should be preserved by his means, when he was cut off from it, and carried far away, and not even reckoned among the living.

Nor did any hope of his liberation remain, especially from the time in which he was neglected by the chief butler. But being condemned to perpetual imprisonment, he was left there to rot. God, however, by such complicated methods, accomplishes what he had purposed.

In this history, we have not only a most beautiful example of divine providence, but also two other points are added especially worthy of notice: first, that the Lord performs his work by wonderful and unusual methods; and, secondly, that he brings forth the salvation of his church, not from magnificent splendour, but from death and the grave. In the person of Joseph, a lively image of Christ is presented.

Apply

Does thinking about how God worked in the life of Joseph and of Christ help you to trust him with the ups and downs of your own life?

What points of comparison and points of difference are there between Christ and Joseph?

Pray

Praise God for his providential guiding of history, and of our own lives.

Ask God to help you trust him, whether life is good at the moment for you, or not.

Notes and Prayers

✻ Day 19 ✻

Joseph Flees Temptation

Genesis 39

Let the faithful endeavour to live upright lives and prudently guard against every mark of evil, even if they must therefore endure the infamy of the world.

Read Genesis 39

Why was Joseph always so successful, wherever he ended up?

Why does he resist the temptation placed before him by Potiphar's wife?

God's Blessing

Let us learn, even amidst our sufferings, to perceive the grace of God. That grace shone forth in Joseph, in no common or usual manner. How base is our ingratitude if we do not refer all our prosperous events to God as their author, seeing that Scripture often teaches us that nothing proceeding from us, whether counsels, or labours, or any means which they can devise, will profit us, unless God gives his blessing.

We are also taught what an advantage it is to give hospitality to the elect children of God, or to join ourselves to those whom the divine favour thus accompanies, that it may spread its fragrance to those who are near them. But we ought above all to centre all our wishes on this one point, that God may be propitious to us.

Beauty and Integrity

We see here how many dangers those who excel in beauty are exposed to; for it is very difficult for them to restrain themselves from all lustful desires. Nothing is easier than for all our senses to infect our minds with depraved desires, unless we are very earnestly on our guard. For Satan never ceases diligently to suggest those things which may incite us to sin. So, let everyone endeavour carefully to govern their eyes, and their ears, and the other members of their body, unless they wish to open so many doors to Satan, into the innermost affections of their heart.

Joseph's constancy is commended. A real fear of God reigned in his mind. He chose to sacrifice his dignity, and was prepared to relinquish life itself, rather than to be guilty of wickedness before God. Seeing that the Spirit of God proposes to us such an example in a youth, what excuse does he leave for men and women of mature age, if they voluntarily throw themselves into sin, or fall into it by a light temptation?

May regard for God alone prevail to subdue all carnal affections. And may we more highly value a good and upright conscience than all the plaudits of the world.

Apply

Do you think your successes in this life are partly down to you and partly down to God's blessing?

How can you cultivate in advance the kind of integrity Joseph showed, so that if a crisis moment arises you are ready to respond in a godly way?

Pray

Thank God for all the blessings of this life which you enjoy, and give him all the credit for any recent successes.

Ask God to help you 'control your own body in a way that is holy and honourable, not in passionate lust like the pagans, who do not know God' (1 Thessalonians 4:4–5).

NOTES AND PRAYERS

※ Day 20 ※

God Meant It for Good

GENESIS 50:15–21

Whatever poison Satan produces, God turns it into medicine for his elect people. Let us adoringly rejoice in this mystery, even if it is beyond our comprehension.

Read Genesis 50:15–21

How has God turned the brothers' evil desires into good for his people (verse 20)?

Does that mean that God sanctions evil?

Am I in Place of God?

Joseph considers the providence of God, and so imposes it on himself as a compulsory law, not only to grant pardon, but also to exercise generosity. Seeing that, by the secret counsel of God, he was led into Egypt for the purpose of preserving the life of his brethren, Joseph must devote himself to this object, lest he should resist God. In effect, he says, 'Since God has deposited your life with me, I should be engaged in war against him, if I were not to be the faithful dispenser of the grace which he had committed to my hands.'

You Meant to Harm Me

Joseph skilfully ascribes the government of all things to God, in a way that preserves the divine administration free from contracting any stain from our vices. The selling of Joseph was a crime detestable for its cruelty and treachery – yet he was not sold except by the decree of heaven. Thus we may say with truth and propriety that Joseph was sold by the wicked consent of his brethren, and by the secret providence of God. While they are contriving the destruction of their brother, God is effecting their deliverance from on high.

Yet it was not a work common to both, in the sense that God sanctioned anything connected with or relating to their wickedness. Nothing is done without God's will, because he governs human counsels, sways their wills, and regulates all events. But if people undertake anything right and just, he so actuates and moves them inwardly by his Spirit, that whatever is good in them may justly be said to come from him.

If Satan and the ungodly rage, he acts by their hands in such an inexpressible manner, that the wickedness and blame of the deed belongs to them alone. For they are not induced to sin, as the faithful are to act aright by the impulse of the Spirit – they are the authors of their own evil, and follow Satan as their leader. The justice of God shines brightly in the midst of the darkness of our sin.

Apply

What would you say to someone who said God was responsible for all the evil in the world, and for not sorting it out with his 'supposedly' unlimited power?

Look back over the whole of Genesis; how has God transformed evil and turned it to good?

Pray

Praise God that he is in such control of the world that he can bring good out of evil without being contaminated by evil himself.

Ask God to help you trust his sovereign control and submit to his will, whether you can see how it's going to turn out or not.

Notes and Prayers

Looking for your next Bible study?

REFLECTING ON
Psalms

with John Calvin

Calvin serves the Church with profound wisdom from these precious psalms. Few others can match the astonishing way he combines deep theological depth, real and practical pastoral concern with careful attention to the detail of the text. The fact that Calvin does this with such simplicity and brevity is all the more remarkable. His thoughts in this short volume will help you, like the blessed one in Psalm 1, to meditate on the life-giving word of God.

Benjamin Sargent,
Dean of Chapel at Winchester College

Scripture with the Saints
*Reading the Bible with faithful believers
across the ages*

Church
Society

The First Book of Homilies

HOMILIES

The Church of England's Official Sermons in Modern English

The Homilies were originally published in 1547, to help reform and renew the Church of England in the biblical faith of the Reformation. They unfold the doctrines of scripture, sin, salvation, and Christian living with clarity and verve. This is what makes returning to the Homilies—now, for the first time, updated in modern English—such an invigorating and life-giving thing to do today.

"The dreadful ignorance as to the fundamentals of our holy religion, that almost everywhere abounds amongst the members of our established church, is chiefly owing to our neglect of preaching and putting into their hands the grand doctrines of the Reformation, contained in these Homilies." George Whitefield (1714-1770)

"The Homilies are a pattern of simplicity and godly sincerity. In their mode of stating divine truth, and enforcing it upon the conscience, they never have been excelled by any composition whatever." Charles Simeon (1759-1836)

"Here we have up-to-date language and inspirational content. I commend this book to you as being challenging, educational, readable, relevant, and necessary for all serious Anglicans throughout the world." Bishop Henry Scriven

UK orders direct from Church Society see:
www.churchsociety.org
admin@churchsociety.org | +44 1923 255410

Church Society

EQUIPPING GOD'S
PEOPLE TO LIVE
GOD'S WORD

ISBN: 978-1-7399376-0-7

offering strategic leadership

For more than 180 years, Church Society has been contending to reform and renew the Church of England in biblical faith, on the basis of its Reformed foundations as expressed in the doctrine of the Articles, the worship of the Prayer Book, and the ministry of the Ordinal.

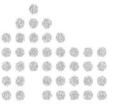

Church Society

To find out more and to join Church Society, please visit our website, churchsociety.org

resourcing today's church

Church Society publishes several new books each year, bringing the best of our Anglican Evangelical heritage to new generations, and responding to new pressures and opportunities in today's Church and nation. We also produce a weekly podcast, a quarterly magazine and a theological journal, as well as our regular blog.

serving tomorrow's church

As part of our commitment to raising up a new generation of leaders, we host the annual Junior Anglican Evangelical Conference for those in the early stages of ministry. Church Society also has patronage of around 130 parishes, helping to protect evangelical ministry in the Church of England for the future.

www.ingramcontent.com/pod-product-compliance
Lightning Source LLC
Chambersburg PA
CBHW040246010526
44119CB00057B/833